W9-BCG-598

To:

From :

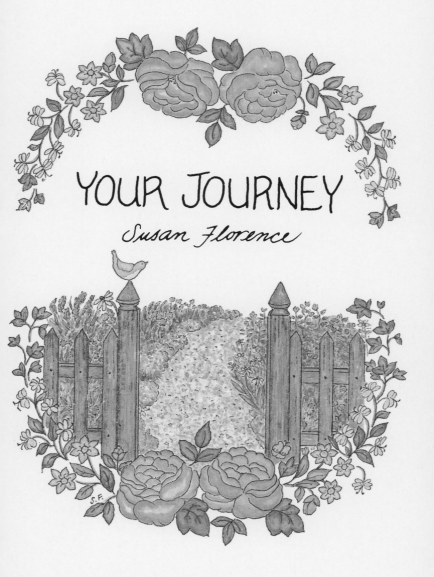

# YOUR JOURNEY

*Susan Florence*

The C.R. Gibson Company, Norwalk, Ct. 06856

There is a journey
    awaiting you.

It comes in truth
    and promise ...
when you reach the point
    of not knowing
    who you are
        or
    where to go.

This most precious
but often painful passage
is the journey
to yourself.

You will travel to places
never before visited,
where you meet
        unspoken fears
and unearth
        buried truths.

You will climb high
and perilous mountains ...
those that rise up
from inside yourself.

You will explore
forgotten waters
held deep in the sea
of your soul.

You will be stranded
in the wilderness
and find a way
through pathless land.

You will be lost
before you are found.

You will be empty
before you are full.

You will cry
the deep sobs of the earth
and tears of rain
will cleanse the house
around your heart.

In time...
because life
like birth and death
knows its own time...

your fears
and struggles
and unknowing
will be transformed.

You will become
a mountain place
where eagles soar.

You will become
a reflecting pool
which sees and knows
the mysteries
of your life.

Your heart
will be light
like a butterfly
as you follow
the currents
of its true desires.

The flight
of the honeybee
will be yours
as you seek the nectar
of what brings sweetness
to your daily life.

Most of all
you will become
who you truly are.

Your life will hold
truth
and promise
and meaning.

And the heart
of the heavens
will hold your heart.